Baby-Fresh Blankets

2

6

9

12

Baby-Fresh Blankets • 1

Beautiful-in-Blue
Baby Afghan

Design provided courtesy of Spinrite

Remember the freshness of gingham fabric? You can get the same look with this charming afghan.

Skill Level
■■□□ EASY

Finished Size
33 x 41 inches

Materials
- Bernat Softee Baby light (light worsted) weight yarn: 13 oz/1,000 yds/360g #31301 his jeans ombré 5 oz/455 yds/140g each #02000 white and #30184 baby denim
- Size G/6/4mm crochet hook or size needed to obtain gauge
- Tapestry needle

3 LIGHT

Gauge
4 dc = 1 inch; 3 sc and 3 dc rows = 2 inches

Pattern Note
Push all treble crochet to right side of work.

Special Stitch
Reverse single crochet (reverse sc): Working from left to right *(see illustration)*, insert hook in next st to the right, complete as sc.

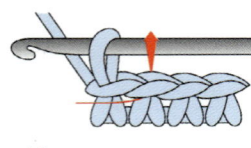

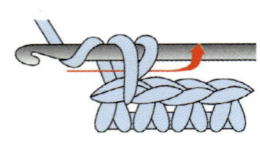

2 • Baby-Fresh Blankets

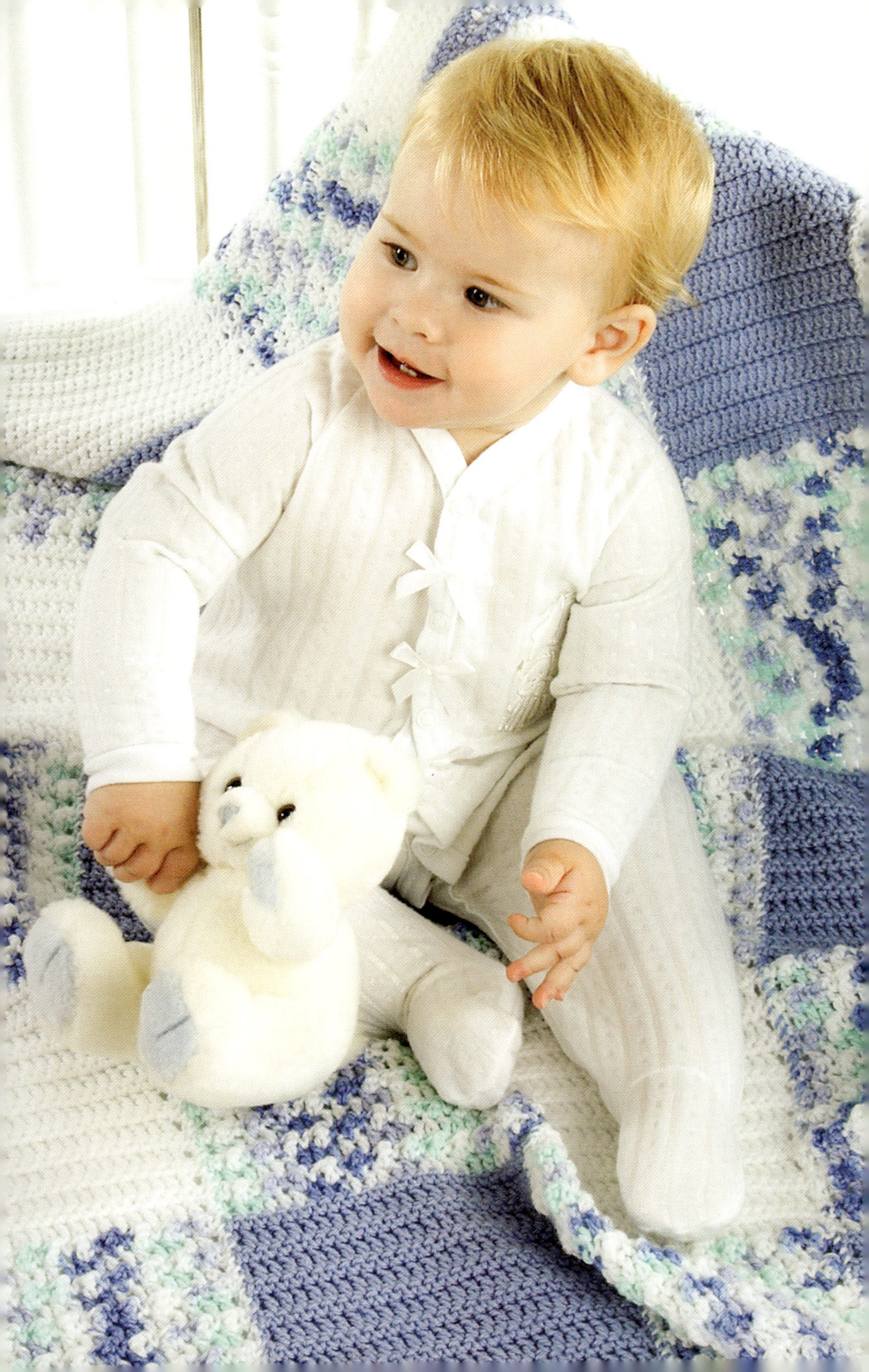

First Panel
Make 3.
Row 1 (RS): With his jeans, ch 27, dc in 4th ch from hook and in each ch across, turn. *(25 dc)*
Row 2: Ch 1, sc in first st, [tr in next st, sc in next st] across, turn.
Row 3: Ch 3 *(counts as first dc)*, dc in each st cross, turn.
Rows 4–18: Rep rows 2 and 3 alternately, ending with row 2. Fasten off at end of last row.
Row 19: Join white with sl st in first st, ch 3, dc in each st across, turn.
Row 20: Ch 1, sc in each st across, turn.
Row 21: Ch 3, dc in each st across, turn.
Rows 22–36: Rep rows 20 and 21 alternately, ending with row 20. Fasten off at end of last row.
Row 37: Join his jeans with sl st in first st, ch 3, dc in each st across, turn.
Rows 38–108: Rep rows 2–37 consecutively, ending with row 36.

2nd Panel
Make 2.
Row 1: With baby denim, ch 27, dc in 4th ch from hook and in each ch across, turn. *(25 dc)*
Row 2: Ch 1, sc in each st across, turn.
Row 3: Ch 3, dc in each st across, turn.
Rows 4–18: Rep rows 2 and 3 alternately, ending with row 2. Fasten off at end of last row.
Row 19: Join his jeans with sl st in first st, ch 3, dc in each st across, turn.
Row 20: Ch 1, sc in first st, [tr in next st, sc in next st] across, turn.
Row 21: Ch 3, dc in each st across, turn.
Rows 22–36: Rep rows 20 and 21 alternately, ending with row 20, Fasten off at end of last row.
Rnd 37: Join baby denim with sl st in first st, ch 3, dc in each st across, turn.
Rows 38–108: Rep rows 2–37 consecutively, ending with row 36.

Alternating First and 2nd Panels, with his jeans, sew long edges tog.

Border
Rnd 1: Join baby denim with sc in any st, sc in each st, sc in end of each sc row and 2 sc in end of each dc row around with 3 sc in

each corner st, join with sl st in beg sc.

Rnd 2: Ch 1, sc in each st around with 3 sc in each center corner st, join with sl st in beg sc, **turn.** Fasten off.

Rnd 3: Join his jeans with sc in any st, tr in next st, [sc in next st, tr in next st] around, join with sl st in beg sc, **turn.** Fasten off.

Rnd 4: Join baby denim with sc in any st, sc in each st around with 3 sc in each center corner st, join with sl st in beg sc.

Rnd 5: Ch 1, working from left to right, **reverse sc** *(see Special Stitch)* in each st around, join with sl st in beg sc. Fasten off. ∎

Rainbow Nap-ghan

Design by Frances Hughes

Treat your toddler to a rainbow of color.

Skill Level
EASY

Finished Size
42 x 45 inches

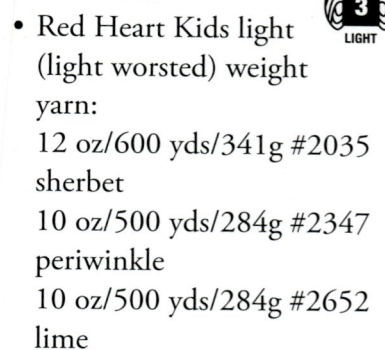

Materials
- Red Heart Kids light (light worsted) weight yarn:
  12 oz/600 yds/341g #2035 sherbet
  10 oz/500 yds/284g #2347 periwinkle
  10 oz/500 yds/284g #2652 lime
- Size 0/2.50mm steel crochet hook or size needed to obtain gauge
- Tapestry needle

Gauge
3 sts = 1 inch; 3 sc rows = ¾ inch.

Pattern Notes
Join with a slip stitch unless otherwise stated.
Beginning chain-3 counts as first double crochet.
Beginning chain-2 counts as first half double crochet.

Special Stitches
Cross-Stitch (cross st): Sk next st, dc in next st; working in front of dc just made, dc in sk st.

Cluster (cl): Yo, insert hook in next st, yo, pull lp through, yo, pull through 2 lps on hook, [yo, insert hook in same st, yo, pull lp through, yo, pull through 2 lps on hook] twice, yo, pull through all 4 lps on hook.

Nap-ghan
Row 1 (RS): With sherbet, ch

121, sc in 2nd ch from hook and in each ch across, turn. *(120 sc)*

Row 2: Ch 1, sc in each st across, turn.

Row 3: Ch 1, sc in each st across, **do not turn.** Fasten off.

Row 4 (RS): Join lime in first st, ch 3, **cross st** *(see Special Stitches)* across to last st, dc in last st, **do not turn.** Fasten off. *(59 cross sts, 2 dc)*

Row 5: Join lime with sc in first st, sc in each st across, **do not turn.** Fasten off. *(120 sc)*

Rows 6–8: Rep rows 4 and 5 alternately, ending with row 4.

Row 9: Join sherbet with sc in first st, sc in each st across, turn. *(120 sc)*

Baby-Fresh Blankets • 7

Rows 10 & 11: Rep rows 2 and 3.
Row 12: Join periwinkle in first st, ch 2, hdc in each st across, turn. *(120 hdc)*
Row 13: Ch 3, dc in each st across, turn. *(120 dc)*
Row 14 (RS): Ch 4 *(counts as first dc and ch-1 sp)*, sk next st, **cl** *(see Special Stitches)* in next st, [ch 1, sk next st, cl in next st] across to last st, dc in last st, turn. *(59 cls, 59 ch sps, 2 dc)*
Row 15: Ch 3, dc in each st and in each ch across, turn. *(120 dc)*
Row 16: Ch 2, hdc in each st across, **do not turn.** Fasten off. *(120 hdc)*
Row 17: Join sherbet with sc in first st, sc in each st across, turn. *(120 sc)*
Rows 18–91: Rep rows 2–17 consecutively, ending with row 11.

Edging

Rnd 1 (RS): Join periwinkle with sc in first st, sc in each st across with 3 sc in last st, working in ends of rows, evenly sp 150 sc across; working in starting ch on opposite side of row 1, 3 sc in first ch, sc in each ch across with 3 sc in last ch, working in ends of rows, evenly sp 150 sc across, 2 sc in same st as beg sc, join in beg sc, **turn.** Fasten off. *(548 sc)*
Rnd 2 (WS): Join sherbet with sl st in any st, ch 2, hdc in each st around with 3 hdc in each center corner st, join in 2nd ch of beg ch-2, **do not turn.** *(556 hdc)*
Rnd 3: Ch 3, dc in each st around with 3 dc in each center corner st, join in 3rd ch of beg ch-3, **do not turn.** Fasten off. *(564 dc)*
Rnd 4: Join sherbet in any center corner st, ch 3, (cl, ch 1, cl) in same st, *[ch 1, sk next st, cl in next st] across to 2 sts before next center corner st**, (cl, ch 1, cl) in next center corner st, rep from * around, ending last rep at **, join in beg cl, **turn.** *(284 cls)*
Rnd 5 (RS): Ch 1, sc in first cl, ch 4, [sc in top of next cl, ch 4] around, join in beg sc, **do not turn.** Fasten off.
Rnd 6: Join lime with sc in any ch sp, 2 sc in same sp, 3 sc in each ch sp around, join in beg sc. Fasten off. ∎

Lavender
Lace Baby Afghan

Design by Hilary C. Murphy

An elaborate edging of love knots and picots accents a simple seed stitch body to create the beautiful detail and wonderful texture of this precious baby blanket.

Skill Level
■■■□ INTERMEDIATE

Finished Size
35 x 41 inches

Materials
- Bernat Baby Coordinates light (light worsted) weight yarn (6 oz/471 yds/170g per ball): 3 balls #01010 soft mauve
- Size H/8/5mm crochet hook or size needed to obtain gauge

Gauge
9 sc and 8 ch-1 sps = 4 inches; 18 rows = 14 inches

Special Stitches
Love knot: Pull up ¾-inch lp on hook, yo, pull lp through, sc in back strand of long lp *(see illustration, Figs. 1–3 on page 14)*.

Double love knot: *Pull up ¾-inch lp on hook *(see Fig. 1)*, yo, pull lp through, sc in back strand of long lp *(see Figs. 2 and 3)*, rep from * *(see Figs. 4 and 5 on page 14)*.

Picot: Ch 3, sc in top of last st made.

Afghan
Row 1: Ch 120 loosely, sc in 2nd ch from hook, [ch 1, sk next ch, sc in next ch] across, turn. *(60 sc, 59 ch-1 sps)*

Row 2: Ch 1, sc in first st, sc in next ch-1 sp, [ch 1, sk next st, sc in next ch-1 sp] across to last st, sc in last st, turn.

Row 3: Ch 1, sc in first st, [ch 1, sk next st, sc in next ch-1 sp]

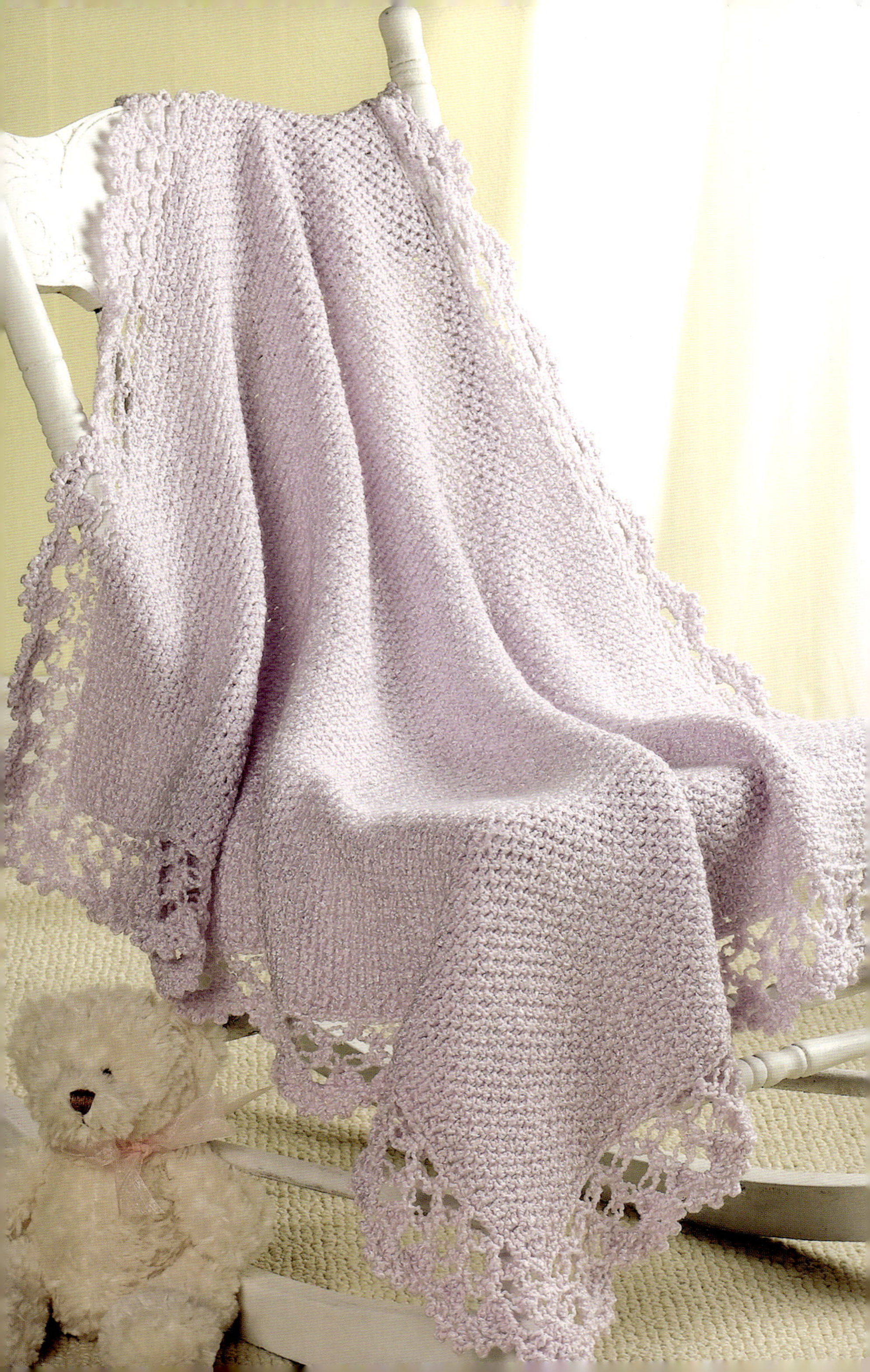

across to last 2 sts, ch 1, sk next st, sc in last st, turn.
Next rows: Rep rows 2 and 3 alternately until piece measures 34 inches. **Do not fasten off.**

Border

Rnd 1: Ch 1, 2 sc in first st, *evenly sp 89 sc across to next corner, 3 sc in next corner, evenly sp 105 sc across to next corner*, 3 sc in next corner, working in starting ch on opposite side of row 1, rep between * once, sc in same st as beg sc, join with sl st in beg sc. *(400 sc)*

Rnd 2: Ch 1, sc in first st, [**double love knot** *(see Special Stitches)*, sk next 3 sts, sc in next st] around to last 3 sts, double love knot, sk last 3 sts, join with sl st in beg sc.

Rnd 3: Ch 5 *(counts as first tr and ch-1 sp)*, tr in same st, ***love knot** *(see Special Stitches)*, sc in center sc of next double love knot, [double love knot, sc in center sc of next double love knot] 22 times, love knot, (tr, ch 1, tr) in next sc, love knot, sc in center sc of next double love knot, [double love knot, sc in center sc of next double love knot] 26 times, love knot*, (tr, ch 1, tr) in next sc, rep between * once, join with sl st in 4th ch of beg ch-5.

Rnd 4: Sl st in next ch-1 sp, ch 3 *(counts as first dc)*, 5 dc in same sp, *ch 3, [4 dc in center sc of next double love knot, ch 1] 21 times, 4 dc in center sc of next double love knot, ch 3, 6 dc in next corner ch-1 sp, ch 3, [4 dc in center sc of next double love knot, ch 1] 25 times, 4 dc in center sc of next double love knot, ch 3*, 6 dc in next corner ch-1 sp, rep between * once, join with sl st in 3rd ch of beg ch-3.

Rnd 5: Ch 6, sc in 3rd ch from hook *(counts as first dc and picot)*, ch 1, (dc, **picot**—*see Special Stitches*, ch 1) in each of next 4 sts, (dc, picot) in next st, sc in next ch-3 sp *[(dc, picot) 5 times in next ch-1 sp, sc in next ch-1 sp] 10 times, (dc, picot) 5 times in next ch-1 sp, sc in next ch-3 sp, (dc, picot, ch 1) in each of next 5 dc, (dc, picot) in next dc, sc in next ch-3 sp, [(dc, picot) 5 times in next ch-1 sp, sc in next ch-1 sp] 12 times, (dc, picot) 5 times in next ch-1 sp, sc in next ch-3 sp*, (dc, picot, ch 1) in each of next 5 dc, (dc, picot) in next dc, sc in next ch-3 sp, rep between * once, join with sl st in 3rd ch of beg ch-6. Fasten off. ∎

Cotton Candy Stripes

Design by Aline Suplinskas

Dainty, textured stitches worked in pretty pastel stripes make this sweet little blanket as cute as it is cuddly!

Skill Level
EASY

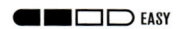

Finished Size
32 x 41 inches

Materials
- Fine (baby) weight yarn:
  10½ oz/954 yds/298g white
  1¾ oz/159 yds/50g each turquoise, yellow, green and blue
- Size G/6/4mm crochet hook or size needed to obtain gauge

Gauge
9 sts = 2 inches; 3 sc rows and 2 dc rows = 2 inches

Pattern Notes
Beginning chain-3 counts as first double crochet.
Work over white when not in use and pick up when needed.

Blanket
Row 1 (RS): With white, ch 143, dc in 4th ch from hook and in each ch across, **changing color** *(see Stitch Guide on page 15)* to turquoise in last st made, turn. Drop white. *(141 dc)*

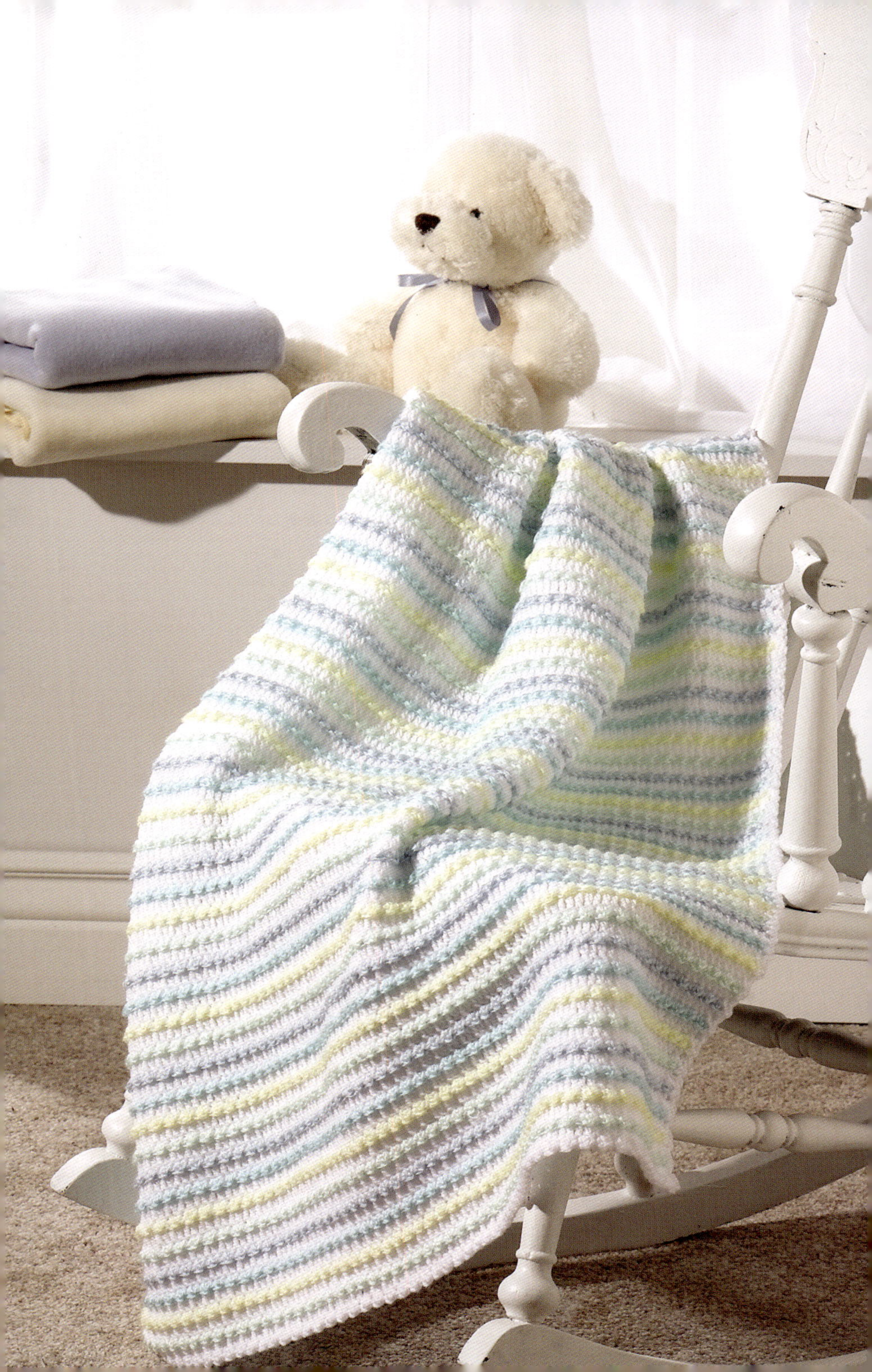

Row 2: Ch 1, sl st in first st, [dc in next st, sl st in next st] across, turn. Fasten off turquoise. Pick up white. *(71 sl sts, 70 dc)*

Row 3: Working this row in **back lps** *(see Stitch Guide on page 15)*, ch 3, dc in each st across, changing to yellow in last st made. Drop white. *(141 dc)*

Row 4: Ch 1, sl st in first st, [dc in next st, sl st in next st] across, turn. Fasten off yellow. Pick up white. *(71 sl sts, 70 dc)*

Rows 5–110: Working in color sequence of green/white, blue/white, turquoise/white and yellow/white, rep rows 3 and 4 alternately.

Row 111: Working this row in back lps, ch 3, dc in each st across, turn. *(141 dc)*

Rnd 112: Now working in rnds, ch 1, sl st in first st, dc in next st, [sl st in next st or in end of next row, dc in next st or in end of next row] around with (sl st, dc) in each corner, join with sl st in beg sl st. Fasten off. ■

Double Love Knot

Fig. 1:

Fig. 2:

Fig. 3:

Fig. 4:

Fig. 5:

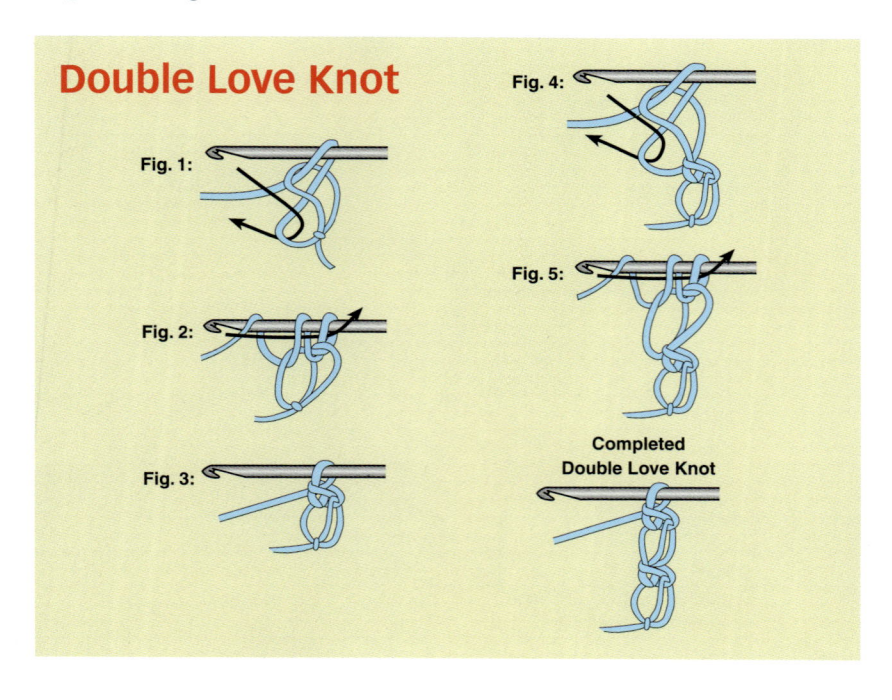

Completed Double Love Knot

Stitch Guide

Chain—ch: Yo, pull through lp on hook.

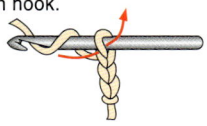

Slip stitch—sl st: Insert hook in st, yo, pull through both lps on hook.

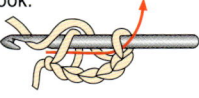

Single crochet—sc: Insert hook in st, yo, pull through st, yo, pull through both lps on hook.

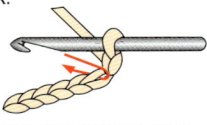

Half double crochet—hdc: Yo, insert hook in st, yo, pull through st, yo, pull through all 3 lps on hook.

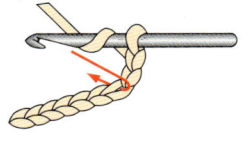

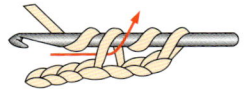

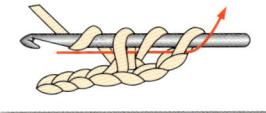

Change colors: Drop first color; with 2nd color, pull through last 2 lps of st.

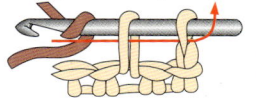

Double crochet—dc: Yo, insert hook in st, yo, pull through st, [yo, pull through 2 lps on hook] twice.

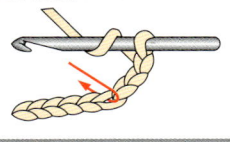

Treble crochet—tr: Yo twice, insert hook in st, yo, pull through st, [yo, pull through 2 lps on hook] 3 times.

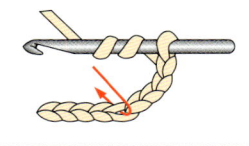

Double treble crochet—dtr: Yo 3 times, insert hook in st, yo, pull through st, [yo, pull through 2 lps on hook] 4 times.

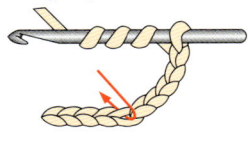

Front loop—front lp
Back loop—back lp

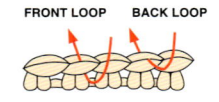

FRONT LOOP   BACK LOOP

Front post stitch—fp:
Back post stitch—bp: When working post st, insert hook from right to left around post of st on previous row.

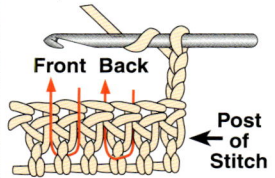

Front   Back

Post of Stitch

Single crochet decrease (sc dec): (Insert hook, yo, draw up a lp) in each of the sts indicated, yo, draw through all lps on hook.

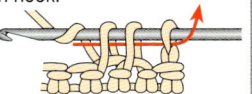

Example of 2-sc dec

Half double crochet decrease (hdc dec): (Yo, insert hook, yo, draw lp through) in each of the sts indicated, yo, draw through all lps on hook.

Example of 2-hdc dec

Double crochet decrease (dc dec): (Yo, insert hook, yo, draw lp through, yo, draw through 2 lps on hook) in each of the sts indicated, yo, draw through all lps on hook.

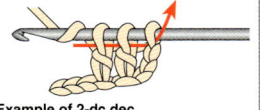

Example of 2-dc dec

ABBREVIATIONS

beg .... begin/beginning
bpdc .... back post double crochet
bpsc .... back post single crochet
bptr .... back post treble crochet
CC .... contrasting color
ch .... chain stitch
ch- .... refers to chain or space previously made (i.e., ch-1 space)
ch sp .... chain space
cl .... cluster
cm .... centimeter(s)
dc .... double crochet
dec .... decrease/decreases/decreasing
dtr .... double treble crochet
fpdc .... front post double crochet
fpsc .... front post single crochet
fptr .... front post treble crochet
g .... gram(s)
hdc .... half double crochet
inc .... increase/increases/increasing
lp(s) .... loop(s)
MC .... main color
mm .... millimeter(s)
oz .... ounce(s)
pc .... popcorn
rem .... remain/remaining
rep .... repeat(s)
rnd(s) .... round(s)
RS .... right side
sc .... single crochet
sk .... skip(ped)
sl st .... slip stitch
sp(s) .... space(s)
st(s) .... stitch(es)
tog .... together
tr .... treble crochet
trtr .... triple treble
WS .... wrong side
yd(s) .... yard(s)
yo .... yarn over

STANDARD YARN WEIGHT SYSTEM

Categories of yarn, gauge ranges, and recommended hook sizes.

Yarn Weight Symbol & Category Names	1 SUPER FINE	2 FINE	3 LIGHT	4 MEDIUM	5 BULKY	6 SUPER BULKY
Type of Yarns in Category	Sock, Fingering, Baby	Sport, Baby	DK, Light Worsted	Worsted, Afghan, Aran	Chunky, Craft, Rug	Super Chunky, Roving
Crochet Gauge* Ranges in Single Crochet to 4 inch	21–32 sts	16–20 sts	12–17 sts	11–14 sts	8–11 sts	5–9 sts
Recommended Hook in Metric Size Range	2.25–3.25mm	3.5–4.5mm	4.5–5.5mm	5.5–6.5mm	6.5–9mm	9mm and larger
Recommended Hook– U.S. Size Range	B1–E4	E4–7	7–I9	I9–K10½	K10½–M13	M13 and larger

*Guidelines only: The above reflect the most commonly used gauges and hook sizes for specific yarn categories.

Skill Levels

BEGINNER
Beginner projects using basic stitches. Minimal shaping.

INTERMEDIATE
Projects with a variety of stitches, mid-level shaping and finishing.

EASY
Projects using basic stitches, repetitive stitch patterns, simple color changes and simple shaping and finishing.

EXPERIENCED
Projects using advanced techniques and stitches, more intricate lace patterns and numerous color changes.

Baby-Fresh Blankets © 2004, 2005 House of White Birches, 306 East Parr Road, Berne, IN 46711, (260) 589-4000. Customer_Service@whitebirches.com.

This publication is protected under federal copyright laws. All rights reserved. Reproduction or distribution of this publication, or any other House of White Birches or Leisure Arts publication, including publications which are out of print, is prohibited unless specifically authorized. This includes, but is not limited to, any form of reproduction or distribution on or through the Internet, including posting, scanning and e-mail transmission.

We have made every effort to ensure that the instructions in this book are complete and accurate. We cannot be responsible for human error, typographical mistakes or variations in individual work. The designs in this book are protected by copyright; however, you may make the designs for your personal use. This right is surpassed when the designs are made by employees or sold commercially.

Published by Leisure Arts, Inc., 104 Champs Blvd., STE 100, Maumelle, AR 72113-6738, www.leisurearts.com.